Our Weird Re

Martyn Crucefix is a British poet and translator, the author of eight original collections of poetry, including *Between a Drowning Man* (Salt, 2023) and *Cargo of Limbs* (Hercules Editions, 2019). A chapbook, *Walking Away*, is published by Dare-Gale Press. Crucefix has received an Eric Gregory award, a Hawthornden Fellowship, and the Schlegel-Tieck Prize for his translations (from the German) of poems by Peter Huchel, published by Shearsman Books. His translation of Rainer Maria Rilke's *Duino Elegies* (Enitharmon, 2006) was shortlisted for the Popescu Prize for Poetry Translation. His translations of essays by German poet and novelist, Lutz Seiler, *In Case of Loss*, are published by And Other Stories, and a major Rilke Selected Poems, *Change Your Life*, is published by Pushkin Press (2024). His new translation of Jürgen Becker's 1993 collection, *Foxtrot at the Erfurt Stadium* is published by Shearsman Books in 2026. Till recently, Crucefix was a Royal Literary Fund Fellow at The British Library and he edits the Acumen Poetry Magazine Young Poets web page. Blog and website at http://www.martyncrucefix.com

Also by Martyn Crucefix

Poetry

Walking Away (Dare-Gale Press, 2025)
Between a Drowning Man (Salt Books, 2023)
Cargo of Limbs (Hercules Editions, 2019)
The Lovely Disciplines (Seren Books, 2017)
O. at the Edge of the Gorge (Guillemot Press, 2017)
A Convoy (If A Leaf Falls Press, 2017)
A Hatfield Mass (Worple Press, 2014)
The Time We Turned (Shearsman Books, 2014)
Hurt (Enitharmon Press, 2010)
An English Nazareth (Enitharmon Press, 2004)
A Madder Ghost (Enitharmon Press, 1997)
On Whistler Mountain (Sinclair-Stevenson, 1994)
At The Mountjoy Hotel (Enitharmon Press, 1993)
Beneath Tremendous Rain (Enitharmon Press, 1990)

Translations

Jürgen Becker: *Foxtrot in the Erfurt Stadium* (Shearsman Books, 2026)
Rainer Maria Rilke: *Change Your Life* (Pushkin Press, 2024)
Lutz Seiler: *In Case of Loss* – essays (And Other Stories, 2023)
Peter Huchel: *These Numbered Days* (Shearsman Books, 2019)
Daodejing – versions of the Chinese classic (Enitharmon Press, 2016)
Rainer Maria Rilke: *Sonnets to Orpheus* (Enitharmon Press, 2012)
Rainer Maria Rilke: *Duino Elegies* (Enitharmon Press, 2006)

Our Weird Regiment

Martyn Crucefix

Shearsman Books

First published in the United Kingdom in 2026 by
Shearsman Books
PO Box 4239
Swindon
SN3 9FN

Shearsman Books Ltd Registered Office
30–31 St. James Place, Mangotsfield, Bristol BS16 9JB
(this address not for correspondence)

EU AUTHORISED REPRESENTATIVE:
Lightning Source France
1 Av. Johannes Gutenberg, 78310 Maurepas, France
Email: compliance@lightningsource.fr

www.shearsman.com

ISBN 978-1-83738-005-3

Contents

'make music and work at it' (*Phaedo*)

'...to hope till Hope creates
From its own wreck the thing it contemplates'
(Shelley, *Prometheus Unbound*)

Heal Thyself

This one believed
I maybe had the brains
another that I had
the right demeanour

but the Schools denied me
till it was too late
then reprieved me
with the offer of a place

that by then I knew
I could not refuse
(such anticipation
had struck such roots)

so I've no recall
of the moment of choice
before those appalling
digs in Eltham

where I had to stow
my dislocated skeleton
by the bed—crammed
one side of my head

with tendons muscles
and pharmacol
with biochem and
bright nets of nerves

everything spilling out
the other side
into failure—fallen
to wandering streets

to stealing Everyman's
Selected Wordsworth
I was John Stuart Mill
hoping my soul

might be saved I felt
love etiolating
the girl from home
now a girl from home

her kisses like shrugs
at London Bridge
saying go your own way
at least not imposed

not merely allowed
and if you want to live
deliberately first
you slit the shroud

1

Ida Belle

Ping

I can talk of course
  but mostly listen
and at lunchtime
  snowflakes crashing down

onto London tarmac
  though you'd hardly
describe this as snow
  not even sleet

yet something more
  fleecy than hailstones
making a noise
  in the instant of falling

a kind of shuffling
  one thing on another
as the waitress runs
  to the plate-glass door

where she holds out
  her mobile phone
for just a moment
  and presses record

because it's there—
  this strange rustling
swoosh—and worth it
  this muttering noise

gets whatsapped
  to her older sister
an exclamatory caption
  pings on her phone

where it lies face down
  on a cluttered desk
gazing for a moment
  up at the clouds

where they drift over
  Manchester's river
warily she stops
  what she's at to listen

How to Send a Plain Dispatch

Hemingway dodged snipers and shells
here in nineteen-thirty-nine

making his way up the Gran Via
to the Telefónica building

intent on filing his plain dispatches—
now lines of taxis shimmer here

each flaunting the official livery
of a blood-red stripe on a white ground

like ambulances—each one purrs
nothing can be simply what it declares

Stepping Out

A breeze blows up as the pressure drops
  and there's something wrong
with the steps ahead
              though a jaunty tub
            of scarlet geraniums
              wriggles its flowers to and fro

but start at the top where a few begin
  where the treads and risers
appear level and steady
              though if you set out
            from down below you face
              instead this lop-sided grin

this prospect of roughened stones
  tipped and tilting
beneath dressed slabs rising
              straight and apparently true
            (yet splashed with lichen
              as with sickness—yellow—white—

or is it nothing but paint
  daubed and spilled
by some earlier child)—yet step
              if you dare and halfway down
            the right side's faulted
              if you set out from above

though if you started from below
  you'll catch a glimpse
of sealing cement dabbed here

and there on the left
where slant treads appear
affected by frost or summer rain

though perhaps each riser rakes
left as much as right
to make balance awkward
yet some fleeting grace
in having come so far (or
the breeze) makes you look back

with your feet at the summit
from whence you return
into the garden or if you began
above then up to where a tub
of scarlet geraniums
spills its petals on the ground

Descent from White Hill

Come down at dusk
  from the mountain passes
a mountain moon
  my sole companion

glance over my shoulder
  at the path taken
hardly a gleam of blue
  under the skyline

a thread-bare blue
  but you grasp my hand
on the last incline
  lead me to your house

where there are children
  quick to draw down
rose-bloom blinds
  against the running briar

frugally we eat
  then we each carry
uncertain candles
  to the damp backyard

where whips of new growth
  honeysuckle
stoop low to bless
  the traveller's head

such pleasure in a place
  of peacefulness
you bring out red wine
  you pour it freely

we each take turns
  to sing to the breeze
as it finds its way
  through the silver birch

till our songs are done
  the Milky Way pales
and I am drunk
  (though no more than you)

and there is nothing
  we know left to spoil
our brief forgetfulness
  of that other world

Other People's Parties

I can't count how many times I've walked out of them,
not even making my excuses. That we're *apart* from
all other things, he says, the *mythos*
of the individuated self, she says, she gave birth
to a full-grown woman, when she was already
fifty-three. In the far kitchen, along the hallway,
outside the bathroom, the eavesdropped fragments
of other people's conversations (always more interesting
than the slow plod of your own with the man
wearing a blue neckerchief). A clicking in her womb,
unmistakably, how it felt. Pulling the blue door,
the cream door, the apartment door,
the church hall door, gently to, and then turning

into the lovely falling rain, or with a glance at Orion
in the night sky, the length of a suburban street
with its privet hedges. She spent the whole day
on her own cake, gluing it together with sweet
chocolate paste, each baked and carefully sliced bar
of sponge in different colours laid side
by side, entombed in icing to create a variegated
surprise. Even from my own birthday party,
the noise swelling within, I turned from the door
and took hold of your hand and we travelled
roads we named to our own *déjeuner sur l'herbe,*
where we were fortunate to find children playing.

Men Working Overhead

Under the pink knitted hat of the gazing child,
  a look of wonder up into the tree; let her be
the one who grows up, marries, comes south, plants
  a sapling in her back garden that fifty years on
is carefully recorded in the council's planning
  decision to permit the felling of *a fine specimen*
of red-leaved acer palmatum; looking at the tree,
  instead, I see calculations of balance, mass,
movement, assessments of trunk and branch by
  girth and length, new varieties of protective
gear, the constant (risks of) gravity's drag; there's
  a young girl across the street, new arrivals,
leant from the front bedroom window, she watches
  strange people pass below, pointing them out
to her father who has one arm round her waist
  (the risks of gravity), the other hand absently
touching his bearded chin. Today, the hard hats
  being worn are blue, the nylon harness red, hi-vis
gilets are yellow, and these are first steps, since
  it's colour that earths us, the start of autumn,
leaves being shaken loose, the greyish brown
  of bark, the shocking yellow of a tree's exposed,
weeping inner flesh. I married the daughter
  of that northern girl; for years we saw the acer
leaf and fall; today I sit here in her father's
  leather armchair, watching a girl at the window,
pointing and talking; the eyes beneath the pink
  knitted hat turned back to the man swinging
high in a tree on red nylon ropes and pulleys,
  in short rasps his saw cutting branch on branch
of shaking leaves, with a shouted warning, moments

before a thumb on the ground; the child's now
ready to take her next step, I hear her saying,
does it hurt the tree, the next close on behind,
at the next thump and cry: what is it trees feel?

The Pantanal

home to 463 species of birds, 269 species of fish, more than 236 species of mammals, 141 species of reptiles and amphibians, and over 9,000 subspecies of invertebrates

The resting actor (his back towards me)
wrestles with the gleaming Gaggia's
steam wand so it takes ages
to get served—the woman before me
in a creased brown dress looks at the cakes

which are brightly lit under the glass
as for a gala performance then orders
a mint tea and a glass of tap water
what the doctor's prescribed
are walks at pace and Birkenstocks

but before that the plan's to retrace
the path across the width of heath:
scorched earth—on three inches of screen—
the Pantanal ablaze and a sentence
to read then re-read: *the skeletons*

of alligators lie lifeless and charred—
all familiar words yet I've never
seen them in that order before
(so a kind of poetry)—the man at my back
in a dark suit is white and middle-aged

smiling and (wearing clothes like that)
he'll be working the law to someone's
advantage (the actor with a ponytail
quickly serves him) and a spokesman
for a local NGO can be heard using the word

‘vanish’ as transitive verb as in
the risks are from wildfires vanishing
the planet—through the door to the street
yellow warning lights on a works lorry
unloading pipes for a longstanding leak:

round here water runs like filthy money
not downhill but into people’s pockets
onto higher ground onto the green lawns
of fenced communities beyond signs
that say *These Gates Are Alarmed*

Anniversary

2040

You lean closer though my eyes are elsewhere
slyly off to where the sun is falling
up the empty beach past the high dunes

and beyond the dunes the shape of pines
where there's still a little shade to be had
where years back we spread a red blanket

to eat and drink and stare at the ocean
(the waters of which were still possible then
the sun's skin-scorch no more than that)

and squads of gulls above soupy waves—
I have a picture stashed away still
of Mum and Dad when they were younger

than I am now showing pink and white flesh
in their skimpy bathing costumes
and he's leaning close to her as she lies

with her toes and knees together—happy
you can tell—oh so happy—beside them
slumps an old-style tartan duffle bag

and I've come down for their anniversary
thinking I might risk the open air
for the advisory thirty minutes or so

my own flesh covered with an oilskin mac
a mask of sorts (and this dried holdfast
of long-dead kelp some fool idea from

a dark web page) and away you stagger
in pursuit of my floppy-brimmed gleaming
hat where it's been blown off by a gust

under skies fading today that bay green-blue
which is strange still yet almost beautiful
and the longer I lie here the more lethal

Salisbury (short let)

In the year of the election, in early June,
  the third year of the war, the four of us
woken—we thought—by the whinnying
  of horses; architecture with a sense
of irony: we find the best (least obstructed)
  view of the famous cathedral's from
the top deck of the multi-storey: through
  a wall, the shrieking of women; beyond
the wooden lap fence, the grumbling
  of working men under a tall oak tree.
Once, coming back, two deer in the field
  below the house: that look (of being looked at),
that stiffening of muscle (sensing
  the stiffening of muscle); the horses, too,
turned out to be real, though why they cried
  we never knew—maybe, being fed,
or a whip being taken to them, not really
  apocalyptic, but a distant rhyme
with the world as it appeared that year.
  In bed, later, you said we ought to think
of the deer as heralding hope, at once,
  walking into the green of growing maize.

How to Listen In

A vast rust-red beast
  overlooks the mountains
where late snows sketch
  gullies and depressions

the lake water is cold
  deep dark and freezing
and the trees are talking
  amongst themselves

speaking to the ground
  once you were mother
and black earth responds
  I am sister I am brother

and on bare green rock
  a handful of moisture
christens the lakeside
  with the notion of cure

and nothing is aloof
  though knives in hands
carve definitive edges
  for ease of handling

yet nothing true to beast
  to blue crag or trees
all pale thighs and elbows
  lifting their leaves

above a heat-struck sky
  above linearity
the earth's complex song
  still buoys the city

Zoological Society of London

Today they are weighing the inmates of the zoo
          and must lure them onto the scales
with fish or fruit or seeds or scraps of meat
          because they are not happy to be coerced
to squat or stand or slump on their sides
          while the telling needles quiver to a stop
to still all this rebelliousness of life—
          the penguins will not peaceably queue
and antelopes shy and shiver out of line
          pawing the dirt of their enclosures
as parrots tip defiant heads already heavily armed
          with nut-cracking bills sensing a fight
in the offing and indeed from all sides
          there's a shriek a growl a roar
though if you enquire of the green-jacketed keepers
          they're sure it's done for the animals' good
yet the pygmy hippo remains unconvinced
          and drowns herself deeper and the flamingos hide
under pink wings and the guys in green
          are possessed of no sweet voice or powerful lyre
so camels continue to peel back their jagger lips
          showing filthy teeth the big cats hunker down
and it seems the bald-headed eagle cannot resist
          the eviscerated rat left to ooze on the scales
and by lunchtime half the penguins have been

          freed back into their pool's oily glint
and progress has been made on the colobus monkeys
          (but slowly they are so difficult to catch)
and the monitor lizard can
          really only be *invited* to come forward

to stroll across the waiting scales
        the black bear thankfully is sleepy enough
in her improvised sling and perhaps
        she hardly knows what they are doing to her
and it's not clear to me if the great shoals of fins
        are reduced to kilos or whether clouds of wings
are assessed in their thousands
        to be converted to individuals
by some pre-set programme or smart algorithm
        but fascinating so much blood scale horn
flesh and bone must eventually
        come chattering from the banks of printers
till finally the busy day's weary twilight falls
        and a breeze rises to blow sheets of newsprint
past the gorillas' empty cages
        the headline seen—then lost—seen again
in a tumbling litany into the distance
        permitting glimpses only of a report
from the Gale Crater on the Martian surface
        where the probe 'Curiosity' has been weighing dust

Don't Cry, Ida Belle

The bicycle with no wheels rumbles beneath me
so I've no need to look
to where I am going
(and there is nowhere I've been today)
the attic window view seems unchanging
though storm clouds gather
on the horizon behind me
swept in despite our primitive wish
to name the weather
like an acquaintance we hope to gain influence over
so then *Hi! Christoph!*
though he has left the roof
above me undampened for yet a while

and though it's his advance that is flicking on
the yellow lights I look down upon
while Robert Johnson fills my ears
with the last fair deal going down
don't cry—Ida Belle—this time
as a President's exit leaves the President
to address a regimented field of flags
a field of stones I imagine raised
and shaking on the killing floors
where Howlin' Wolf (and I) stir a blues heat

in which I alone manage the virtual miles
of my exercise bike's
piled stacks of Lego-like bricks
composing my day's attainable goals
before tonight's downtrodden sand
and before tomorrow's breaking news

that Christoph burst the banks of the Dee
(exactly as was predicted)
felled trees to the east of Wrexham
cut off twenty villages beyond Holt
the newsreader's precise naming of names
not her first (or our last) illusion of control

Olly and Pepper Are Safe

Rectangular blue shapes on the pavement
like dying moths under his feet,
the trampled dead, their blue upper wings
the pale white over which he walks
through the hospital's rolling doors
feeling more than a little delirious

at last as he leaves another double shift
in the rammed ICU: the bleeps, the shallow
laboured breathing, the emptying beds
cleared swiftly as a busy table service;
emerging now he must shield his eyes
with that morning's unread newspaper

against the glare of streetlights
against the foggy black of a frosty night
and the dazzling fireflies of raised phones
over the hats and heads of what he takes
to be relatives, a group of grieving people;
they are shouting some sort of refusal

his weariness makes it hard to grasp;
they come bumping and pushing close,
they bellow even in each other's faces,
in his face, their chance to trample masks
on the pavement, to swing a placard
into the face of this wicked thing

even, from a tired doctor's hand, to knock
a colluding newspaper in which a page
of unread home news reports:

two newborn toms pulled from a bin liner
on a conveyor belt to the recycling crusher;
thank goodness there were eagle-eyes,

thank God some action was swiftly taken,
firm assurances beneath the headline
that the pair will now be hand-reared,
given names in a process of adoption,
concerned officials issuing statements:
there are never enough kittens in the news.

Electric Clippers

Fleecy Disney Christmas snowflakes fall
  so the street's quiet is even more muffled
than usual but for the creak of boots
  my own and my son's and he's telling me
his numbers (as men will do—as I did
  enough times with my own father too)
the work numbers he's posted this month
  despite lockdown and how his new boss
is shaping up 'better than expected'
  and all the while we walk he gathers
above his strong brow like a jutting roof
  a little shelf of snow on the dark fringe
he's been compelled to grow (the barber
  on the Broadway out of action for weeks)
and we've agreed he'll come and get it fixed

so he's bought and brought electric clippers
  and back home we hurry through the house
to the garden—a black garden chair
  set out under the snowfall—and there
I drive a firm plough up and over his scalp
  through thick young dark hair that falls
in clumps over the deepening snow
  to lie like the darkest of brushstrokes
and after ten minutes you might imagine
  the foxes had returned the previous night
for larger prey and torn it to pieces
  then we're done—both shivering now—
back through the house and perhaps
  a quick complicit grin goes between us
though unseen behind our baby-blue masks

How to Address the Inquiry

If he was still in his armchair beside me
            I guess I'd try to raise a smile—
            perhaps, for want of better, with this tale
of last night's troubled tossing in bed
            one arm snagging the bedside lamp

to bring it *thump* onto the bridge of my nose
            to leave a bleb of dried blood
            in the mirror this morning proving
I fought and lost—or else I might
            tease him with his beloved City

in the fight for relegation again
            or perhaps I'd pull back the curtain
            you see there! a few primroses!
or I'd find my phone and maybe show
            the newly done memorial bench

bearing his name by a tree in the park
            and in the quiet I'd hear ashes stir
            a murmuring of lips beyond cracked
and inaudible though I know the gist
            that *I was let down—they're slow to act*

letting people come they let people go
            running it'll be fine! *up their fucking flagpole*
            then backhanding fat cat chums
with a hundred and fifty thousand lives
            a fire sale fobbed me off with shit deals

even dangling one last Christmas before me
only to shove it—old ashy whisperer—
folded into yourself like a dishcloth
on the drainer—a hiccupping cough
into your pillow—a last companion—

too old to ventilate… I've his wedding day
on my fireplace—you should come see
how young they are with what awkward pride
he stands in sunlight at the end of the war
in his mid-twenties in his Air Force uniform

Breakdown Recovery

How long one night in December can seem
  approaching with the narrow rays of the sun
stopped at the roadside waiting for angels to come
  at the Garage Derudet you sit and see day done
through the glass that once flashed *CITROËN*
  where gleaming bodywork and bright chrome shone
but is now the breakdown waiting room
  from which Derudet Père—with the help of his son—
sets out to rescue the halt the broken the lame
  and it's like *Nighthawks*—plate-glass windows the same—
and the late-night road suddenly plies its stream
  of dazzling headlights without interruption
every vehicle assured of its own destination
  as your taxi bill blinks its swiftly rising sum
and now the hotel receptionist's weary grin
  not long before the moon ascends at 2 a.m.
her bone-white arms laid on the black mountain
  beyond which she slips as those imposters come
(the brutal roadside necklaces of sodium
  that flatter to be but cannot be the true dawn)
and crouching blocks of suburbs vanishing
  to be replaced by the murmur and hum
of the airport where you queue up to weigh-in
  (the image of an ageing prize-fighter in decline)
where you fret for hours you shiver and yawn
  (your wheels at the mercy of Derudet and Son)
how long it is till at last you're stumbling
  onto the tarmac where a bird sings unseen
or is it the whistling of the jet engine
  the perfumed early-shift hostess bids you welcome
as landscapes of shadow slide beneath each wing
  at 7,000 feet portals blaze with the risen sun
you say 'how long a night in December can seem'

Civil Disobedience

Craigie & Cuthbert

Twenty-eight days down
a damp black shaft
worming through a criss-cross
of hand-dug tunnels
going down past
knuckle-jointed gas and water pipes
skirting the power cables
and the sewerage
all the subterranean business
that confines us lets us be
(interment as an act of resistance)—
surprised by a face
under a beanie (thirty-one days)
by a chewing stubbled jaw
and a grin sinking back
into the earth with the aim
of protecting it
(thirty-seven days)
the bailiffs gathering
to break open the ground
who was it discovered the body
uncorrupted (forty-nine days)
and nothing but the gulls
and grey views of the North Sea
common seals and their pups
and his holy body
not subject to decomposition
and how was it no-one
recovered the Saxon cross
deep inside his clothes
dragged down by gravity
towards the earth

(seven years in his mouldering chest)
solitary yet at the same time
engagé out of such a life
comes a great miracle
or was it simply
that it had been mislaid
(ten years under his obdurate heart)
there are so many ways
for a saint to stumble
into grace—interment as
an act of resistance—
even beneath Rettendon
where twenty-five years deep
in that blacked-out shaft
a few kilos of matter
set deliberately out of place

Whip Hand

I stoop where they dug
  into the tufa rock
for want of better
  with a ticking of picks
hollowed out over years
  a series of boxes
this ambient temperature
  to last almost forever
then waking under attack—
  imagine—from others
who had even fewer
  possessions their families
holding their breath
  in the labyrinth bolthole
they prayed to live
  to go on selling slag
beyond White Hill
  at crippling prices
to raise the lady's house
  its huge fireplaces
its built wooden roof
  like an over-turned fleet

of turrets and roof-tiles
  of gleaming slate
she grows bored with—
  it's said—so she rides
side-saddle up the steep
  spiral staircase
the horse wide-eyed
  as its shrieking rider

for the thrill of it
  climbing as if pursued
yet the creature cannot
  turn but hooded
cajoled backwards
  by those who serve her
and imagining this
  I will cast myself
cowering in the dark
  with fire to flush them
on the shrilling stairway
  blinded by the hood
or whip in hand
  as proof I'm not dead

2

Flint

Our Weird Regiment

How the rich impress
  with what they own
displaying family photos
  on the piano lid

as if no different
 to us where we shuffle
through elaborate rooms
 or glance aside

through leaded glass
 into formal gardens
where cabbage
 potato and mint perhaps

chive and marjoram
 are elegantly deployed
to be admired
 not cooked or eaten

as our guide explains
 farmland purchased
to the churchyard wall
 and then beyond it

each mound ploughed
 and levelled in accord
with his lordship's
 goose-feathered whim

yet a scattering of bones
 assembles itself
in a heap at the gate
 now beyond the gate

our weird regiment
 lurches into the road
a swaying of skulls
 and whitened knucklebones

Abraham's Bosom

Wells-next-the-Sea

The flints traditionally embedded
in the walls of many of the houses
in this rebel county grow more rounded

the closer you get to the sea; the mudflats,
the inhospitable salt marshes:
through a kissing-gate to the lake, just

a few paces through Corsican and Maritime
and Scots pines and she insists
I take a seat in the arms of the one

laying its vast, elbowed branches
close to the ground as if it wished
to settle them into its own pine straw.

I do as I'm told. I perch on a patch
of rough, scaly bark, swinging my feet
inches off the ground and, finding it

more comfortable than I'd expected,
lean back as in an armchair, impaling
my neck, a fatal injury, on a razor-

cut, broken, pine branch behind me,
sharp as the point of a pike: the weapon
of choice in the defence of democracy.

A Gastarbeiter Cleans the Big House

Norfolk, England, 2030

It was the English woman Veronica Berridge
who let the place go—her spirit
          vanishing maybe eight years back
          I imagine into one of these portraits
in the top room perhaps this—which I like—
          composed for the most part of bare canvas

her features as I stare seeming to surface
from a natural ground from beneath
          the halo of the nocturne of her hair
          though she'd more years on her than this
and more trouble over which to draw
          an English veil—it can hardly resemble her

yet this broad face the curve of her lips
the hooded side-glancing eyes urge me on
          in the absence of other information—
          I've heard she was a plantswoman
and a devoted mother and often
          at this high west-facing window she'd stand

to view the large kidney-shaped garden pond
its tall flags inclined in the faint breeze
          her box-hedge borders her rose-beds
          the rudbeckia the frothing bridal lace
the twisted apple tree leant into the cherry
          and with each Spring these two queens

would break into riotous blossoming
as each sequential child foundered and died
          she took to walking—I imagine—

the paths or here at this clumsy portrait
as if before a mirror though in fact I see
her differently—more palely consumptive—

and perhaps the truth is the house let *her* go
(a strange unwarranted act of compassion)
and who now thinks of Veronica Berridge
sees an ageing childless English widow
and no-one but me ever comes to stand
at this ruby-lipped portrait on which I gaze
imagining children under the flowering trees

How to Talk to the Children

When will we learn with the morning rush
to get ourselves our things out the door
compelled only by the pushy clock
not boots on the streets who'll ask who
or what we are—by what authority
by what right—instead this scrum
for books and shoes and mobile phones
and nothing proves easy to find—then
it's hard to avoid the accusatory tone

(as this morning I sent you both back
to scour bedside tables and beneath clothes
beyond each door in the cluttered dreck
of each brightening space)—then
it is hard to blame the behaviour
not the child—*you had it last night*
then ran out back with your bags
and now you've no idea where it's gone
so check the pockets of your coat again
and listen—remember—what I always say
how all things get carelessly left
in the obvious place—well don't they—
so look in the pile on the dresser shelf

and *ta-dah!* what's lost waits patiently there—
just a moment before chaos resumes
our interrupted dash to the door
compelled only by hands of this or that clock
(not boots on the streets who'd lean in
close demanding who or what we are
who are always so quick to learn
how to exploit predictable behaviours

whose power depends on how alert we are
to the narrowing gulf between
life lived in jeopardy and life secure)

Late Assyrian Kings

after Housman

On White Hill every street's in trouble
as the October woods shrug
and seem not to care
storms outside and storms inside squall
beneath a blizzard of news
nor do you even dare to believe
any have known this before
yet Ashurbanipal was once
master absolute and his demise
we've let slip into time's long drain
that swills harder faster—O
what skilful youthful bowman's mother
stood in such delight back then
before some paradisal scene
quite sure this would last forever
as we wish yet guess as much
that we are of such deluded green
in hope maladroit as the woods riot—
and the dark woods too—
the bough-splitting gales rake
and destroy and we reply
in spite (even as our heartlands
go up for sale) we cry—surely—surely—
we'll survive such tempests
(we know enough to poison the air!)
yet boys and girls who quarrel
and flirt in far other tongues will—
rest assured—soon be walking here

Muzzle

Monitory figures holding white flags aloft
          at intervals along the field boundary
                    moving as one towards the hanging wood
          with their backs turned
                    they do not glance at us
where we walk the two nearer men wave
                    their signals—but not at us—you wonder
          I'm inclined to whisper but not for long
as we descend through autumn fields
                              into the noise of birds flapping—perhaps
                    because of us—a few leaves
          already spoiling green to orange and amber

we turn down under the wooded cliff-face
                    following a clearly waymarked path
                    into a shooting party of grizzle-headed men
all pockets and steadily up-turned
          looks—though not at us—motionless
                              high into the rockface
                    twenty of them necks craned into the woods
          their slim black guns cocked and ready

and thunderously one downs
          a flapping escapee we hear the sound
of something landing heavily somewhere
                    and cannot take our eyes from
                    the smoking barrel—though not for us—
yet waving us on along the narrow track
          through their established lines
beneath the cliff-face where two push on
                    unconsidered a circle of 4x4s

parked below the *crack crack* of shots behind us
no burr of human sound
not even our own words
as we emerge onto ploughland a thickset dog

is crouched beside a man gazing at us
impatient unscathed now the dog
cantilevers up onto all fours at a swift-dropping shape
beyond the treeline and the man
shifts his weight the muzzle of his gun
almost touching the dog's alert ears
his throat rattles with as much discipline as it requires

Quick Ornithological Quiz

And so yesterday's right answer was cock
 not inclined to colourful clothing
 and cock's choice of a mid-range feather
and cocks finding contentment or full of guilt
 alone above the brimming water

and cocks liable to act out like tigers
 cocks preferring to live modestly enough
 while cocks express a liking for patterns
rich and broad as their clamorous wings
 and perhaps any cock on occasion

enjoys isolation yet today's correct answer
 is that cocks tend to favour fruit
 (but are not averse to tackling meat)
that cocks cover great distances at twilight
 (but always find their own way home)

that cocks like to hang with clever people
 (by implication people like themselves)
 though it's true cocks can be common
they are enormously resourceful
 to be honest cocks have such busy minds

(which is why some can be indecisive
 torn between passion and commitment
 no better than crows on black dog days)
and morph then into proper loners
 though if given a tree of a decent height

and once impressed by a reasonable cause
 and if left for a few quiet hours together

a cock can recover an outburst of song
quite un-cock-like though this year's answer
is that cocks are keeping their heads down

expecting storms and so your diary entry
(wishing this year's brood tall in the air
before heaven turns grey before them)
is in error—too many companionable wings
have gone missing—

Masculinity

You've fought this for so long, but comes
  a time when you understand you are second rate,
no more that brightness
  with which you shone, worn thin and opaque

as milk or rather—this is how it goes—
  perhaps it never did glow so brightly,
that boldness with which you addressed the world,
  paled to white feather, all the while,

from your place in the crowd, you attend
  to the blurring of his steps that now
penetrate like a language
  streaming over the dark gulf of the world

to pierce the obscure recesses of the mind,
  through the flimsy tissue we dress ourselves in,
this flattery of beige and green,
  these faddish opinions in scumbled brown

that you used to rehearse ironic jokes about,
  but now you seldom dream of better
and you have still not grasped the point
  of all the books the stats the schedules

the strict diet, the ten thousand hours
  when you tried to pull yourself up to
the topmost drawer, to be the best, instead
  it's enviousness you have bred

in the wake of his glittering, his belling, his roar,
  you've lost out to the swift morse
of his feet, carrying him to the utmost point
  from which, in triumph, you have to listen

to him condescend to you, though even this
  he does with such grace and elan
you just have to smile and take it on the chin,
  nor do you have it in you not to love him.

In the Lantern Tower

Made to shed light
  to keep sailors from harm
then a likely place
  to imprison them

for days for long years
  soft stone carved
with dates and names
  of others and their own

with scores of sketches
  flags and anchors
ships reefed in full sail
  conceived side-on

from their confinement—
  no scrawled woman
one cock and balls—
  men have nothing to say

but what they know
  the womb-dark sea
ships that brought them
  months of durance

given no sight of home
  till the vessel's the place
where they belong
  under lock and key

no other and no more
  but loss of liberty
men yearn for the tip
  and yaw of the sea.

Come the End of the Working Day

after Breughel

Gazing from the frame as if somebody
  has hollered 'hey look at the birdie boys'
you look great—Hans—with your fat arse
  ballooning like the Christmas season
from those red hose bold as your strong
  straight-arm pull on the rope to secure
the bundle of grey harvested twigs
  you or Nico will stoop to next moment
then hoist up and over your shoulder
  the pair of you hurrying to the village
to the blazing fires at the low tavern
  where Nico will tip up too many jars
(in the hope they'll dull his aching tooth)
  and slyly pull his flute out for the girls

though it's past midwinter's joyful pivot
  and the pair of you glare (look closely)
through the season's wheel of good will
  into—what is this?—mere carelessness
or mischief or a brute malignity
  driving both of you to slip off through
the trees without stopping to call Frans
  who's up there at the top of his ladder
still wielding his conscientious blade
  trimming and letting fall tomorrow's load
of feeble twigs as if his life—the truth!—
  do you really consider him so other
as to be deaf—Nico—to your shrill whistle
  careless—Hans—to your great *basso* call?

Mobile Car Valet

'Before, behind, between, above, below'

1

Like a pair of lovers bored back-to-back in bed
  his white van closes rear bumper to bumper
and he opens the doors starting to squeegee
  the mucky hubs of the big black German

2

from a sudsy bucket he works the dusty body
  with a chamois leather inscribing S-shapes
like a brief foaming of bold graffiti
  around wing mirrors and gleaming roof rails

3

then balanced on a tyre he sweeps half the roof
  now the other inside and across the length
of the dash a pale duster the armrests especially
  working the driver's side and a jet-spray

4

jumps into hissing life spilling gassy whites
  over wings and tyres (it's his best weapon)
stashed in the van then out with the Henry
  its scarlet chess piece and snaking black hose

5

good to scour the seats then into the footwells
  and the chamois again to buff stray drops
on windows with windolene smelling nice to him
  now the doors slam the remote locking chirps

6

as he carries the fob back to the marble foyer
  like a hatchling his van waits out the length
of one smoke no word from the big black German
  up close and glittering already turned away

Prayer Flags

'whenever I have no ideas, I do the washing up'—Durs Grünbein

Listen up, you presidents, kings, prime ministers,
today's a day that ought to begin with chores,
let it start (as it once did, surely will again)
with the washing of the shopping that you brought in
to the house and spread across the floor—
do you remember?—how very well I remember
mornings with a cloth soaked in antibacterial
(no bleach no taint) piece-working my way across a field
of bottles, glass jars, toiletries, tetrapacs,
too much plastic, a light bulb, a few paper bags—
then it's begun—the hoover kicked into full-throated action,
systematically through the kitchen
with the non-toxic surface cleaner which sprays
the smell of clementines (so it claims)
to cut through all kinds of grease and grime,
and so it goes—do you hear this, presidents and prime
ministers, even kings and queens,
should start with equivocal pleasures, virtuous pains,
such as chopping wood, emptying bins, buying your own flowers,
and, as the man warns us, those not familiar
with such routines as often open up new ways
(as turning a line, or a rhyme, resolves the maze)
aye, wide open, there's the paradox,
as if spun off at a wild tangent to your damp cloth's
circular motion as it brightens kitchen surfaces,
there's an opening up of novel vistas,
or the same ones, seen slant, while some other door
slams behind you, not closing down, rather
a new start, you'll see it, considering the prayer flags,
answered, the laundered cleaning rags
hung up—the red, the orange, and the blue—
drying on the radiator in the corner of your room.

The Inheritors

In a café, near a dropped Bonne Maman's
queasy splatter of bright raspberry jam
and glass shards, hearing whispered talk
of ant infestation, the fear of it, in
a house one of the girls doesn't own, but
she lives in now or feels responsible for;
it's complicated, this business of a word
finding its place beside a single meaning,

the act of translating the familiar into
the estranged, eavesdropping. Under the sofa,
a sugary pile, black specks of the dead,
a few scouts from the upper world bring
news: a little forgetful, some joint pain
(psoriatic), but broadly good for his age,
this gentleman it was pleasant to meet
this morning (who talks like that these days?).

O inheritance, disease, taxes coming due,
nature denatured, the shock of care home fees:
all these are gifts we've handed on
to our children and grandchildren; it's jobs
now, failed interviews, working from home,
and ants in Dad's house, where she pops in
to make sure he's milk, and bread, and jam,
the basics, he says, don't you worry now,

with the seasons the buggers come and go
and we have a sort of working arrangement:
they visit, take sackfuls of what they want,
then back to their world from this one, where
I feel less and less at home with these aches

and pains, but it's not as if we've nothing
to talk about, I think it's no more than
the same world seen from far different ends.

Estrangement

'The herb itself I like not'

I see Old Man thrives in your front yard
  and there's an old man standing
in the front bay window
  of the ground floor flat where since March

you rent the upper with your new partner
  and you're keen to explain
you are living no more than a mile
  from the woman you left last winter

and the daughter you see most afternoons
  though you don't invite her here
where she might stop and pick and sniff
  the grey feathery herb that loves the sun

that loves the parched soil in your yard
  where she might turn in distaste
but remember it well—no—
  she's not to be given the chance to visit

since there are degrees of estrangement
  and each knows it's true—
the unshaven face in the ground floor bay
  staring out to where I toss my keys

shifting to and fro like a restless colt
  I see him smile and I smile back
guessing he hears steps in the room above
  the scrape of a chair as you call goodbye

moments later brushing past grey fronds
  of Lad's Love then a run of lights
turning green as you lean to show me
  the door to which you no longer hold the key

How to Wake Up as Someone Else

First light, in bed, remembering everything
with the weight and clarity
of heraldry—the silk dress,
gules, you wore cut to the thigh,
the neckline a miracle, its reply
to the bristling sunlight—
salient, at the top of the stair,
you found yourself, found you were
free as never before, lifted your chin
as if you'd been summoned
to climb to him—swaying leaves
of that dress, incarnadine,
in motion as slow-bruising fruit—
your slow descent, his stiff shadow
stood far off, where darker curves
engross a dense maze, their roseate
gleam to a laser-straight light:
you close on him in his cramped,
dazzling space—your silence,
the full moon's rise, he can say nothing,
you've already filled his eyes,
first light, in bed, remembering everything.

All Was Sweet

The telegraph wires swept left to right
as far as I recall heading south and the lane
to the rest of the village curved left to right too
as the setting sun dropped to cast this weird orange glow
to daub the grey facade of the house—
the kind of house a child will draw
with one chimney at each gabled end
with its two pairs of windows to either side
of a central porched door the facade fronted
by a low brick wall that stirred itself
only to run each side of the gravelled drive
to reach the height of two low pillars or posts
on the furthest of which you sat waiting for me to retrace
the few yards I'd retreated to take this picture—
and I don't remember how you got there
whether I lifted you mock gallant perhaps
or more likely you essayed your
tom-boyish walk along the wall then
an independent heave and twist and there you sat
your hands clasped between splayed denim thighs
your round face with its ever-expectant look
though it's not possible to see you clearly
since my desire to frame the bend of the road
with the sweep of the wires
above your grandfather's symmetrical house
has set you at such a distance and though the curve
of your back suggests impatience your face
remains no larger your glance towards me
no more legible than the vanishing head of the pin
on which for six sweet months I set angels dancing

Motion and Stillness

for Debra Allbery

In motion these days these distances driven
mean restless nights in unfamiliar beds
in which I drive the long roads again
as during last night I visited you
in the city of Charlottesville
in a room I created largely from glass—
my dreaming machinery's stab at
your home in the eastern United States
its transparencies so literal—

and there I stooped to kiss you chastely
on your cheek while your husband
stood by and my wife was there too
all fully attending—then four of us
moving through the minor French chateau
I visited yesterday with its towers
and its crumbling tufa stone
its population of chafing crickets
its stable yard where two kittens played

the smaller one smudged ginger-white
the other's pelt was of purest white
(the white we're told happiness writes)
and the four of us stopped
and watched as they played at power
and submission each tumbling together
till it was impossible to distinguish
one from another—just the two of us
alone then as we walked awkwardly

from room to room through Keats House
from case to profound glass case
lifting the heavy light-dampers
to read his two-hundred-year-old script
even as you described your home
its position high on Bridgestone Drive
and I replied with mine—its blue front door
its little English gravel yard—
each with no thought of going further
though it may be four hundred miles
tomorrow by dusk perhaps forty years
and each dawn breaking as if to prove
we fall in love with stillness and still we move

3

Homespun

Summers Ended in Sweetness

Under the boughs of the oak named Eve
  a shape settling its wheels into the turf
as if to say sooner or later
  everything will sink like this wish-

bone of an ancient farmyard cart
  this four-wheeled broken-backed wreck
with its inadvertent load of scraps
  in the metal hopper long since blotched

and scorched with rust now peppered
  with acorns and grey twigs
the season's debris from the spreading trees
  and over its bent rear axle sits

a barrel-shaped composite of metal hoops
  bent wooden staves clamped one to another
that years ago proved water-tight
  the wood originally young and full

now shrunken—staves lost wholesale—
  and it was here that baskets of grapes
were brought to be pressed beneath
  the screw wound down to the metal base

until the year's juice spilled from the spout
  protruding like an obscene tongue
upon which decades of summers
  ended in sweetness and towards which gangs

of children inclined their hands only to be
  told to scat to clear out of the way

by their fathers who heaved
  at the wooden cross-struts like a capstan

as they looked to squeeze more and still more
  oozing sweetness to drink or decant
or spill across the ground—
  and now it all stands and rots

the fat metal bolts lie where they dropped
  still others loosening perhaps to fall
in the course of this winter or next
  each heavy square-headed bolt that a child

might gaze at and think it must last
  forever instead lasting just long enough
to be outmoded—till this four-wheeled cart
  came to a halt here one September dusk

left to stand beneath the boughs
  of Adam and Eve while someone hoped
it might prove useful for one more year—
  but they never came back

not the hands and not the baskets
  not the horses and no tractor returned
and no more did the children though they still
  sometimes stir in their sour old age

to stare at hands stiff now and more used
  to the walking frame and smiling
to find wrinkled fingers a little sticky still
  with the taste of six or seven summers

Old Union Songs

for Bruce and Joy

Yesterday a hi-vis orange fringe and rattails
  framing her black lips, black skirt, black nets,
to say: *don't look at me in that way you have,*
  though the quiet carriage went on staring.

Now waking in your spare room, you bring me
  a mug of tea and (not resembling him
in the slightest) you remind me of my father
  when he could climb the stairs with a tray

steady before him, no need of the banister…
  Defiance! We practice it now, when what's
possible narrows, the world's presumption
  narrowing more quickly. Now breakfast

in your back room: charms at the bird table,
  roses redefine arch as arbour, the brick
privy a locked bike shed, accompanied
  by old union songs, three-part harmonies,

a bodhran, a fiddle, Joy leading the way.
  Years ago, you both came to my wedding.
In my speech I said I'd wed the Ptolemy
  girl's 'infinite variety'. I think so still,

though time chews away at what we do.
  Then we are agreed? A firm defiance?
Cleo's black bangs more grizzled now.
  Joy grins: *an orange quiff? or bright lippy?*

Ten Yellows for Helen Kidd

When the forsythia in your backyard bloomed,
  and beyond leaf-fall, it was Kidlington where
we gathered, the anxious writers, come out of town
  to find you in the chaos of your three-child house.
I picked my way to a chair through charity shop
  bric-a-brac I found were treasured possessions.
Big as snowflakes, stars outside, inspirational,
  if we were in the mood to be inspired. Never,
to your face, of course, but did we find something
  reassuringly *maternal* there? On a train, you'd
compose a rough-hewn poem: see it in Spring,
  say it by Summer, sorted by snowfall. I cried
in your living room once, over the Yellow Pages.
  Was it the sight of your son, Tom, his shock
of straw-blond hair, arriving home from school?
  Impossible to say what moved me, impossible,
as it was then when you had the tact not to ask.
  You said, listen to this track, you'll love it:
the album unpromisingly called 'Parachutes',
  when we wanted the youthful thrill of free fall.
Inexplicable, tears like stars falling, skin and bone

  made salt water. Released, my phone tells me
in seconds, at the millennium, much later than
  unreliable memory suggests. On my cheeks,
tears… on the table, the bottle of burnt-
yellow Irish after midnight. Framed, your arms
  linked at Greenham's yellow gate. Back then,
I saw more of my brother, the train crawling past
  the coal-fired station at Ratcliffe-on-Soar, soon
to be decommissioned. Yet, look how they shine,

the may blossom's out, your children grown
and you dead amidst the chaos. I don't know why…
because by then I had a child of my own, a home
of my own, I painted walls magnolia, was loved,
I think I am. A tune, a dying fall we listened to,
then played again, but nothing's resolved until
it finds resolution in a flood of condolences,
daffodils in a vase, your Facebook page now just
a 'Remembering', not updated, a shot of you,
laughing, a hat on your head, on the hat a bird
of prey, its white feathers, yellow tints, browns,
in low sun: how it behaves itself in your presence.

How to Be Yourself

after Breughel

You want me to say I wore the wrong hat
        not the starched white of these other women
        choosing instead the comfortable green
and without really intending to
        they set me down here—or was it perhaps
                I found my own way to this joint stool

at the furthest corner of one of the more
        outlying tables where I tip back beer
        like a man—and they're maybe thinking
my black dress a deliberate challenge
        yet a sensible choice (don't you think?)
                it goes without saying I wish her well

in clogging it to a future of coupledom
        and quarrelling before her smug smile
        I'd wish godspeed though at this distance
from the tumultuous centre of things
        I'd hardly (would I?) make myself heard
                above the wheezing of several bagpipes

the endless clatter of wooden soup bowls
    and I can't help but notice the little bird
    in the rafters unremarked by them all
nodding its head (don't pretend you saw)
    then ruffling, turning, looking to make
                the quick exit it would prefer if it could

Maggots

The woman who has lived alone for years
crosses her bright-lit kitchen to find
a few grains of spilled basmati on the floor
gathered round her old gardening shoes
beside the rubbish bin where she kneels

to clear them—first slipping her fingers
through the straps of the mud-stained shoes
to lift them—animating the grains—
it seems—the impression she gets—
inflating them like a handful of creamy

puffed fragments as if god-like she stirs
them to life rolling and turning
and dipping head-parts along a line
of motion though the only true
direction of travel (her mother once said

in a moment of surprising openness)
is time's arrow's flight making its way
across the floor each waking grain
nods and shrugs towards its goal
reminding her of her brother's illness

brooding somewhere beneath his tongue
and she's revolted by these creatures
on the floor and on her own tongue
the question that no-one ever
answers: what is it, what's all this for?

Hilperton

She lays squeaking polystyrene trays
  along the lawn's edge and
prepares to plant crimson geraniums
  in any well-drained soil

in sun or partial shade
  to grow strong as a litter of mongrels
with tall stems rising above frilled
  and bruise-zoned foliage

lifting buds like curious green shells
  others are like eyelids caught
in the act of blinking petals
  refusing to wait and where she kneels

she tamps the soil and she hears them
  rejoice as each plant races off
to the far end of an English summer
  through days they occupy unaware

of briefer days long obscured
  by blooms that light her way to July
and August and late September
  even October's chill has its red glimmer

My Mother's Care Home Room

(as Cleopatra's monument)

I sit behind door 16
            in a room the size
of my son's student room
            though it's the old
who shelter here
            and from the only chair
I watch the sun's rays
            through the only window
pierce the canopy
            of tall beech trees
that line the park
            beside this building
sunlight through glass
            and across the sill
onto a blue plastic jug
            its blue plastic cup
of barely touched water
            a single birthday card
from her grandchildren
            a Christmas cactus
and her bracelet watch
            catches a glint
and a glint on the foil
            of today's medication
these few objects
            they tell the time
as the sun rakes
            beyond the trees
an Easter Island profile
            gaunt and beaked
propped up in bed

on the plastic-wrapped
single mattress
the rucked-up sheet
of scrolls and shadow
as the sun travels
falling into the west
I keep my vigil
with all the helpless-
ness of a Charmian
at the cooling feet
of her brave Queen
the asp flung down
beneath the only chair
there has ever been

On Southampton Street

after Bertolt Brecht

A mizzling fog on Southampton Street—
  then suddenly a market stall
with its spectral blooms
  under a bare bulb preternaturally lit

a sullen frizz-haired girl cutting stems—
  I'm dumbstruck as one who's found
the thing he was looking for
  here—at arm's length—chrysanthemums—

nothing but them! I blow on stiff fingers
  plunge them into a pocket for coins
but between fumbling silver
  and glancing back up to check the price

scrawled on yellow card it feels as if
  I interrupt myself—a dull under-voice
lifted in bleak remembrance—
  since last night you're not here or any place

Winchelsea

after Millais' 'The Blind Girl'

The girl is blind
  but she's my mother
who'd sit like this
  with a mug of tea

with an attitude
  you'd say of 'relish'
the idea simply
  of just being here

warmth flooding up
  over her brows
with both eyes closed
  better to enjoy

that sensation
  and if I'm right
(that she's big sister)
  then this other girl

is Gwendolen
  (the more outgoing one
who could not help
  but be observing

crows on the meadow
  the cattle grazing
the paths along
  which they've come)

and only yesterday
  my son laughed
as I drank my coffee
  'Just like your mother'

both eyes closed
  though I hardly knew it
and tortoiseshell wings
  lit on my sleeve

After St Augustine

His mother walking
  some straight and narrow
when—before her—
  this thinning man
who smiles and waits
  you'd think with joy
yet at second glance
  sunk within herself

she's consumed with grief
  her boy-son asking
the cause of it—*say*
  why such sorrow—
and it's not because
  he does not know
as in waking life
  without missing a beat

she says *I'm crying*
  for a son he replies
O then take heart—
  because he must—
here on this pathway
  where we've met
here with these smiles
  I am your son—she

stares up and down
  and gazes along
the narrow causeway
  where he's set her

and assuredly
  she then explains
in my dream I
  spoke with an angel

who did not promise
  where my son was
there I might be
  the angel promised
wherever I am
  where I'm laid down
there he would be:
  he would come to me

He Made This

Nearly one hundred
  Manchurian cranes
standing for good luck
  and longevity

greeting the sunrise
  the entire flock
in mountain country
  the tall pine trees

the plum the bamboo
  three companions
for the days of winter
  when summer's gone

in a few weeks
  these naked willows
will be upholstered
  in inches of snow

black and white cranes
  gone—not far off
white egrets now
  print their black feet

into a fall of snow
  where the artist
incorporates
  a near microscopic

solitary narcissus
  as if expressing
shyly a last wish
  not to be forgotten

Homespun

It's in these mountains I hear my father
as he used to talk on the phone before
handing it into my mother's keeping
he'd gaze out the dining-room window
because the sky would give itself to him

the sky required no effort from him
being wholly present simply available
for his participation or comment—
and so he did—that grey clouds had gathered
that blue skies had held that morning

or spots of rain were now marking the glass
and this was the kind of conversation
he offered as it asked almost no recall
of the past or much anticipation
of what was to come but plainly stood there

in homespun—for all other business
he'd hand the phone over to her swiftly
and it's strange being so far from home
hearing his voice under these jagged skies
(at red dawn mostly or raking sunset)

and though his body is so far distant
I know the voice I tried for years to echo
(its elusive tone and uneven cadence)
I listen to learn if I can perhaps still
match myself to his pure present moment

In This Quiet One-way West Country Town

it's closing time where you spent the last years
    of your life in this provincial market town
where you were happiest—it is
    half past five in the afternoon—closing time
in this newbuild town that in recent years
    outran you like the black and white dog
you walked in the evening and on the streets
    (on Duke Street and Castle Street and Fore Street)

it's closing time along the pavements where
    we walk at half past five hand in hand
as you never did with your own father
(hand in hand as the two of us never did either)
and we've no more purpose but to walk the street
    under this first iron stroke of the half hour
as if time paused but still we step out
    to the sight and sound of locks being drawn

the clunk of bolts in their cradles shoved home
    by shop assistants on tiptoe by pretty girls
in the record store—it's Era and Chubb and Yale
    as the café owners bend stiffly down
it's closing time at Jimmy Ladd's (hands red
    with brick dust closing up) and the butchers
the bakers—at James Long memorial masons
    hands white-gloved with today's marble dust

locking doors and the bitch who sold newspapers
    the one who often made you feel small
and old Stokes the florist putting finishing
    touches to the last wreath of the day as now

he knows it's closing time and the pair of us
            listening to the sound of a thousand keys
as they are turned and as many blinds
            firmly drawn interior lights extinguished

your hand slips mine before I've the chance
            to say I'm sorry I was not there to help
(what could I have done but watch as you went)
            feeling you leave me again on Church Walk
under cloudless skies a gull driven too far
            inland to return now that it's closing time
all across this quiet provincial one-way
            west-country town turning for home before dark

The Restoration Process

1

I send the blues and sarsens to a work colleague
because she recently drove this way: in the distance,
beyond middle England drizzle, numberplates
of cars crawling ahead of us, dipped headlights
of the line of slowly on-coming cars; where we
stopped for a break, on a chalkboard, a personalised,
Starbucks *welcome!!* She replies, between emails,
sorry the sun shone for me now wondering
the only bright day for months will it rain forever?
We slow up for a glimpse of the embodiment
of permanence from our rapid, seamless flight
of days, tailbacks in both directions on a stretch
of perfectly clear road. You turn with a look
of disapproval when I start to complain *what is*
it these days, you rent some place for a week
and no-one sees the need to brew a pot of tea,
not a bag in a mug? The stones, even from the road,
through a swilling windscreen, are so big, you ask
how did they do that, and is that more, or less
puzzling than the question *why*? Solstice, in part,
a sort of memorialising too, with each stone
a 25-ton graffito, laboriously daubed to say:
here we lived, we were here, we passed this way.

2

The same drizzle in the car park where we turn
into a welcome from the volunteers; a tapestry
of a 500-year-old knight on horseback, a video

of the restoration process: a woman working
for eighteen months with just a needle and thread.
You say we ought to stop for milk and bread:
the urgent life of the belly, but this is interesting,
how steam is blown through the fabric of the tapestry,
the run-off the colour of weak tea; after six hours
it flows clear as spring water, the results on show
in a dim room, woven armour plates, a long woven
lance, it looks like he once possessed the world.
At the corner shop, a guy running towards me,
his arms out as if herding sheep, a panicked glance
down the aisle, by the air-curtain cooler, a pietà,
two people dressed in black, one woman laid out
on the tiled floor, the other cradling her, looking
anxiously towards me. There's a second message
from my colleague with a photo of her houseplants
blooming with all the attention she's given them.

3

Shouting, he says, I've got to keep the door shut,
my colleague, he says, my colleague's had a fit
(that's the word he uses). Twenty minutes later,
irritable, in trouble too, we try to find the address
of the Airbnb, the directions unclear if you come
from the east and not from the west as they seem
groundlessly to assume. As we drove off, the man
in black, standing at the door, on the steps of Spar,
I could see him shouting into his phone, hopping
to and fro, I guess, to the emergency services,
saying, my colleague, again he says, she's had a fit,
says, I need help, now, yes, help, look, I'm trying!

The Seventy-ninth Tarot Card

artist unknown, c. 1560

After all that, now you deal me this?
  The seventy-ninth tarot card?
After juggler, papess, lightning-struck tower,
  last judgement, the fool, moon, and star?

From the undignified rear end of a horse,
  an armoured knight tumbling down?
You bring me this image to interpret,
  unfolding across a blank, beige ground:

it must mean something catastrophic,
  turning up now, disaster foretold.
See, the triumphant, three-pronged lance
  of whatever it was he sought to oppose,

and the knight's lance, fumbled on impact,
  let slip from his mailed right hand,
his head, an egg inside the beaked helmet,
  is about to collide with the ground.

Yet look at his green, yellow, pink silks,
  where they flap, his jockey colours,
and, falling backwards, his high-kicking legs,
  wrapped in brilliant, sky-blue hose,

his polished, calf-length, black leather boots
  bring drama to the performance.
Now I think this means after the crash
  Sir Knight will dust himself down, bounce

back, all rubber limbs and resilience.
  Juggler, emperor, spun wheel of fortune?
What the tarot is, it transcends itself,
  beyond what's shown lies something else.

A chariot, temperance, two lovers, strength?
  Say *papa* is dead, long live the pope!
After the hanged man, deal me the seventy-ninth,
  in which against all odds I find hope.

Things Newborn

You can almost see the crisp cellophane
          from the shop still round them: red-streaked
carnations in a vase, on a desk, for our arrival;
          beneath the traffic at Wadebridge, a glint
                    of the crooked river (the Camel), making

its way to the sea at Stepper Point; last night,
          on the next table, a family of five (or was
one the invited boyfriend?), mother and father
          worn thin, the teens bright and nervy at such
                    an enforced, strange occasion, to be faced

without phones; the flowers are a nice touch,
          in truth, they focus, a magnet for the filings
of mind, of scattered memory, some lines
          from *The Winter's Tale*; after a journey,
                    conversation grows stilted, even awkward.

Then pick up a pen. After a long drive, orientation
          is difficult: staring from a window
at the river, across the ring road, a Travelodge
          this way, a neighbour's untidy garden the other;
                    then, as if from an unpromising, forced bud,

waking, a bloom, a way of expressing things
          like catching sight of one of the teenagers,
no, two of them, phones cradled in their laps,
          under napkins, hidden below the lip
                    of the formal table, sly, their energies earthed.

The Adoration of the Kings

after Breughel

Everything looks rough-hewn and doltish
  and has done so since my eyes
began to betray me unreliably now I peer
  through thick blue saucers of glass

yet feel how these strangers stir us—
  this one with the pinched face of a carpenter
more than a king though the bold red
  of his sleeves and collar and the aureate bowl

his fingers dandle appear to be rich indeed
  and quite out of place in our stable yard
where we find this squalling child
  reluctant and bollock-naked as far as I see

then this older one with his lank grey hair
  stooping as if to show off his ermine trim
and his extraordinarily long pink sleeves
  (I see them more clearly than anything else)

he positions his hat and mace in the dirt
  to offer something I can't make out
beside me the black skin and sharp leather smell
  of the third who proffers an elaborate gift

of green and yellow—it must be gold and jade
  yet smells sweetly of spices to me
a sort of sweetness like nothing I've known
  and I can tell you I'm good with odours

even better with my ears which are sharp enough
  to trace the munching commentary
of the ass in the byre the shifting of the crowd
  and the hiss of doltish Piet with his lips

to the poor father's ear telling him I suppose
  what we all know of the difference
in their ages and the ominous signs
  from the fractious boy even the fact the child

cannot possibly be his—shit-for-brains Piet
  in his green snood has never been one to look
beyond the obvious not one to let gossip
  go abegging yet the mother's face has

turned now half-obscured as if she wants us
  to believe there's something in all this
not the sighted nor the blind can fathom
  some secret she and her strangers are keeping

Marking a Zero

1

More than midway now into our journey
          I turn off to the liquid splash of gravel
          under the tyres as we glide to a halt
beneath two poplar trees stirring their heads
          in the stiffening breeze
                    singing with thousands of green tongues

2

interrupted by the slamming of four car doors
          and my son stretching his cramped limbs
          enraptured by the falling of the sun
the fluttering of the quick-coming darkness
          he cries out how he loves to hear
                    the cicadas with their whirring nearby

3

and though I'm already halfway to the house
          I stop and turn back to look
          at where he points to the noise
where it swells under a rosebush—now
          a second speck—and then a third
                    each unremittingly marking the zero

4

of itself with a sound it seems my ears
          can no longer hear (however much
          I strain from the monastic cell
I find myself in) though I protest
          I can make out—far off and faint—
                    the ringing of bells in their stone towers

5

that I can trace their ebb and shimmer
folded through the interference of the breeze
yet he hardly believes me—the cicadas
are so clear to him it's as if it's his own
surprise and shocking loss that I can
hear nothing of the singing in the grass

Acknowledgements and Notes

Thanks to the editors of magazines, websites and anthologies in which earlier versions of some of these poems have appeared: *Agenda; Black Box Manifold; Dreich Magazine; Finished Creatures; The Friday Poem; Glasgow Review of Books; The High Window; Littoral Magazine; The London Magazine; Magma; The Manhattan Review (USA); Modron; Poetry Scotland; Raceme; Riggwelter; Shearsman; Stand; Strix; Tears in the Fence; Temenos Academy Review; The North; Under the Radar; Visual Verse; Wild Court.*

Heal Thyself – was first published in *The London Magazine* and later included in *Poets in Person,* ed. Aprilia Zank (Indigo Dreams, 2014).

Stepping Out – was short-listed in the Live Canon International Poetry Prize 2022 and first published in the Live Canon Anthology (Live Canon, 2022).

Descent from White Hill – is an English version of Li Po's poem 'Coming Down from Chung-Nan Mountain by Hu-Szu's Hermitage', which can be found in *Li Po and Tu Fu,* tr. Arthur Cooper (Penguin Classics, 1973).

Men Working Overhead – was first published on the Lancaster Lit-Fest 2025 website as part of their World Into Words poetry map and was chosen to be read at The World Into Words Gala Poetry Reading, curated and hosted by Litfest's Poet in Residence, Malika Booker in March 2025.

How to listen in – was selected for the Morecombe Poetry Festival Anthology 2025.

Zoological Society of London – was first published in *For the Silent,* ed. Ronnie Goodyer (Indigo Dreams/League Against Cruel Sports, 2019).

Olly and Pepper Are Safe – was commended in the Troubadour International Poetry Prize 2023 (judges Mona Arshi and Tom Sleigh) and appeared on their website: https://www.coffeehousepoetry.org/poems/troubadour-international-poetry-prize-2023

Electric Clippers – an earlier version of this poem first appeared in the 2023 Candlestick Press chapbook, *Christmas Walk: Twelve Poems for Rosy Cheeks.*

Whip Hand – an earlier version of this poem was first published online by *New Boots and Pantisocracies – 100 days of poetry for the austere generation.*

Our Weird Regiment – first published in *Hollow Palaces: an anthology of modern country house poems,* eds. Kevin Gardner and John Greening (Liverpool University Press, 2021).

How to Talk to the Children – was long-listed in the Live Canon International Poetry Prize 2020 and first published in the Live Canon Anthology (Live Canon, 2020).

Late Assyrian Kings – is a 'translation' of AE Housman's poem 'On Wenlock Edge', poem 31 from *A Shropshire Lad* (1896).

Quick Ornithological Quiz – was first published in *Masculinity: An anthology of modern voices,* eds. Rick Dove, Aaron Kent & Stuart McPherson (Broken Sleep Books, 2024).

Estrangement – this poem draws on many details and phrases from Edward Thomas's 1914 poem, 'Old Man'.

Summers Ended in Sweetness – was first featured in the Arachne Press DUSK project in December 2017 and later published in *DUSK,* ed. Cherry Potts (Arachne Press, 2018).

Maggots – was Highly Commended in the Winchester Poetry Prize 2025, judged by Fiona Benson, and published in the anthology *The Lantern Room* (Winchester Poetry Festival, 2025).

My Mother's Care Home Room – was first published in the chapbook *Walking Away* (Dare-Gale Press, 2025).

On Southampton Street – is an English version of Bertolt Brecht's 1934 poem 'Der Orangenkauf', one of his 'English Sonnets' probably addressed to Margarete Steffin. Many thanks to David Constantine for introducing me to this poem.

After St Augustine – is a version of a prose passage from Book 3 of St. Augustine's *Confessions.*

Homespun – was originally published in the anthology *Hiraeth,* edited by Ceda Parkinson and published in 2021 by the micro-press Overneath Books.

In This Quiet One-Way West Country Town – was first published in the chapbook *Walking Away* (Dare-Gale Press, 2025).

The Adoration of the Kings – was first published in *Spring of the Muses: the poetry of music, art and dance,* ed. Deborah Gaye (Avalanche Books, 2019). This poem is included in *A Garland of Poems for Christmas,* eds. Martyn Crucefix & Michael Glover (1889 Books, 2022). It also features on the Mary Evans Picture Library website alongside an image of the Breughel painting.

www.ingramcontent.com/pod-product-compliance
Ingram Content Group UK Ltd.
Pitfield, Milton Keynes, MK11 3LW, UK
UKHW040434050126
466575UK00005B/39